Three Mile Island

Other titles in the *American Disasters* series:

The Challenger Disaster
Tragic Space Flight
ISBN 0-7660-1222-0

El Niño & La Niña
Deadly Weather
ISBN 0-7660-1551-3

The Exxon Valdez
Tragic Oil Spill
ISBN 0-7660-1058-9

Fire in Oakland, California
Billion-Dollar Blaze
ISBN 0-7660-1220-4

The Hindenburg Disaster
Doomed Airship
ISBN 0-7660-1554-8

Hurricane Andrew
Nature's Rage
ISBN 0-7660-1057-0

Love Canal
Toxic Waste Tragedy
ISBN 0-7660-1553-X

Mount St. Helens Volcano
Violent Eruption
ISBN 0-7660-1552-1

The Oklahoma City Bombing
Terror in the Heartland
ISBN 0-7660-1061-9

Polio Epidemic
Crippling Virus Outbreak
ISBN 0-7660-1555-6

The Titanic
Disaster at Sea
ISBN 0-7660-1557-2

Tsunami
Monster Waves
ISBN 0-7660-1786-9

The Siege at Waco
Deadly Inferno
ISBN 0-7660-1218-2

The World Trade Center Bombing
Terror in the Towers
ISBN 0-7660-1056-2

Three Mile Island

Nuclear Disaster

Michael D. Cole

Enslow Publishers, Inc.

40 Industrial Road   PO Box 38
Box 398   Aldershot
Berkeley Heights, NJ 07922 Hants GU12 6BP
USA   UK

http://www.enslow.com

Copyright © 2002 by Michael D. Cole

Library of Congress Cataloging-in-Publication Data

Cole, Michael D.
    Three Mile Island : nuclear disaster / Michael D. Cole.
        p. cm.
    ISBN 0-7660-1556-4
    1. Three Mile Island Nuclear Power Plant—Juvenile literature. 2. Nuclear power
plants—Accidents—Pennsylvania—Harrisburg Region—Juvenile literature.
    3. Nuclear energy—Juvenile literature. [1. Three Mile Island Nuclear Power Plant.
    2. Nuclear power plants—Accidents. 3. Nuclear energy.] I. Title.
    TK1345.H37 C65   2001
    363.17'99'0974818—dc21
                                                    00-011263

Printed in the United States of America

10 9 8 7 6 5 4 3 2 1

To Our Readers:
We have done our best to make sure all Internet addresses in this book were active and
appropriate when we went to press. However, the author and the publisher have no
control over and assume no liability for the material available on those Internet sites
or on other Web sites they may link to. Any comments or suggestions can be sent by
e-mail to comments@enslow.com or to the address on the back cover.

Illustration Credits: All courtesy AP/Wide World Photos except p. 12,
courtesy Enslow Publishers, Inc.

Cover Illustration: AP/Wide World Photos.

Contents

1 General Emergency 7

2 The Nuclear Age 9

3 Meltdown 15

4 Crisis and Confusion 23

5 Calming the Crisis 31

6 The Legacy of
Three Mile Island 36

Other Nuclear Accidents 41

Chapter Notes 42

Glossary 45

Further Reading 46

Internet Addresses 47

Index 48

The cooling stacks of Three Mile Island's Unit 2 reactor are shown above. A partial meltdown occurred in the reactor of Unit 2 in March 1979.

CHAPTER 1

General Emergency

People in Dauphin County and the cities of Harrisburg and Middletown, Pennsylvania, were waking up on Wednesday, the morning of March 28, 1979. After a song, the WKBO radio broadcast was interrupted by reporter Mike Pintek.

"There is a general emergency at Metropolitan Edison Company's Three Mile Island nuclear power plant," Pintek said. "A utility spokesman says there is a problem with the feed-water pump." Pintek's report ended with an assurance from officials at Metropolitan Edison that the public was in no danger. But people living in the area were very alarmed.[1]

The Three Mile Island nuclear power plant is on an island in the Susquahanna River. It is two-and-a-half miles south of Middletown, and twelve miles from Harrisburg, the state capital of Pennsylvania. At the time of the crisis, many Americans were still uncomfortable with the idea of using nuclear energy. Much of the public associated the word "nuclear" with bombs and the spread of dangerous radiation. For some, it was hard to believe nuclear energy was safer than burning coal or gas to meet electrical power needs.

The Three Mile Island plant had been in full operation for only three months. Already there had been an accident.

"The minute I heard that there had been an accident at a nuclear facility," Pennsylvania Governor Richard Thornburgh later said, "I knew we were in another dimension."[2]

Part of the problem was that no one fully understood what was happening. Engineers at the plant were trying to find what caused the accident. Officials at Metropolitan Edison were giving conflicting reports about the emergency. Most reporters understood too little about nuclear energy to make good news judgments. As a result, panic was spreading.

Radiation is invisible. You can not see it or smell it. Yet radiation can cause sickness or death to anyone exposed to large amounts of it. The people living near Three Mile Island were very afraid. How much radiation had already leaked from the power plant? How harmful would it be?

Officials at Metropolitan Edison were slow to give the public answers to these questions. To make matters worse, the answers they did give often conflicted with their earlier statements.

The accident at Three Mile Island was a product of the nuclear age. It was a new and complex kind of disaster. It was a threat that no one could actually see and few could understand.

CHAPTER 2

The Nuclear Age

Nuclear power is a tremendous source of energy. The destructive force of atomic bombs made this clear to Americans and others around the world. In 1945, the United States dropped two atomic bombs on Japan. The bombs utterly destroyed the cities of Hiroshima and Nagasaki, and brought World War II to an end.

The following year, President Harry Truman signed the Atomic Energy Act. Scientists and engineers then began pursuing the idea of using nuclear energy for peaceful purposes. Nuclear energy could produce electric power more cleanly and efficiently than burning coal or gas. But the horrors of the atomic bomb led many people to wonder if nuclear energy would be a blessing or a curse.

The public's attitude was partly a result of ignorance. Few people understood how nuclear reactors worked. Understanding how nuclear reactors work requires knowing a few things about nuclear physics.

This huge mushroom cloud was a result of the atomic bomb dropped on Nagasaki, Japan, on August 9, 1945.

First, there is the atom. Atoms are the smallest parts of an element. At the center of every atom is a nucleus made up of protons and neutrons. Each atom also has electrons, which orbit around the nucleus. These parts of an atom are called subatomic particles.

Splitting an atom is called fission. When an atom fissions (or splits), the energy that held it together is released in the form of heat. This process of releasing energy is the basis of nuclear power. It is called nuclear fission.

Fission is accomplished by bombarding the nucleus of an atom with neutrons. The neutrons split the atom, releasing more neutrons, which split more atoms, and so on. This is called a chain reaction. Chain reactions that result from nuclear fission release a great amount of energy.[1]

Uranium is a common nuclear fuel. Nuclear power plants such as the one at Three Mile Island use uranium fuel rods. These fuel rods are held together in the reactor core. Inside the reactor core, the uranium rods give off heat through fission. Pipes carry water past the fissioning uranium. The hot rods turn the water into steam. The pressure from the steam turns the blades of a turbine. The turbine then generates electric power.

The concept of a nuclear power plant is simple enough, but keeping the nuclear reaction under control is not easy. To keep the fissioning uranium stable, a number of control rods are lowered into the core to absorb extra neutrons. This keeps the uranium rods from getting too hot and melting. [2]

As nuclear power plants developed during the 1950s and 1960s, accidents did occur. In 1961, the S-L 1 reactor at Idaho Falls, Idaho, went out of control and ruptured the building. The rupture resulted in a low-level radiation leak. The reactor core at the Enrico Fermi plant near Detroit, Michigan, partially melted in 1966. A fire at the Brown's Ferry plant in Alabama came close to causing another accident.

While the public still had safety concerns in the 1960s and 1970s, other factors helped gain support for nuclear power. In 1973, the Organization of Petroleum Exporting

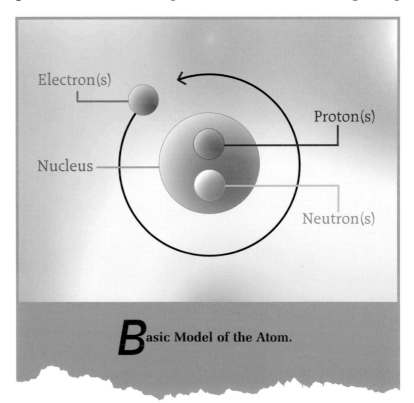

*B*asic Model of the Atom.

Countries (OPEC) decided to cut production and reduce exports of oil to the United States. This made oil much more expensive. This "Energy Crisis" made people realize that dependence on oil could be very costly. Nuclear energy began to look more attractive as an alternative for American energy needs.[3]

Many nuclear power plants were built during the 1970s. One of the companies that built these power plants was the Metropolitan Edison Company, often called "Met Ed" for short. They chose Three Mile Island as the site for a large, two-reactor

President Harry S. Truman signed the Atomic Energy Act in 1946. This encouraged the research of nuclear power as a possible energy resource.

facility. The Babcock & Wilcox company designed the plant. It would provide electrical power to southeastern Pennsylvania.

The Three Mile Island plant was dedicated in September 1978. It began producing energy in January 1979. Within weeks, the reactor was operating at full power.

In the early morning hours of March 28, 1979, a maintenance crew at Three Mile Island was cleaning a filter in reactor Unit 2's cooling system. Filters removed unwanted minerals from the water that was used to produce steam. This water also helped keep the reactor from overheating. Shortly after 4:00 A.M., while the filter was being cleaned, the flow of water was blocked.

The accident had begun.

*B*elow are the huge turbines of the Unit 1 reactor at Three Mile Island, still in use in March 1999. In 1979, a filter in the Unit 2 reactor became blocked, setting off a nuclear crisis.

CHAPTER 3

Meltdown

The blockage in the filter set off an immediate response. Within seconds, automatic systems shut off the steam turbine. This completely stopped the flow of water through the reactor's cooling system. Without water, the temperature in the reactor core quickly rose. If the core became hot enough, the nuclear fuel could melt through the containment structure. This would have released harmful radiation.[1]

At the moment that the turbine was shut off, alarms sounded through Unit 2's control room. Within minutes, hundreds of lights were flashing on the control panels. Operators in the control room tried to cope with the alarms, but there were too many of them, and they were coming too fast.

Control rods were supposed to drop into place, along with a flow of water, in order to lower the temperature in the core. However, one of the valves that released water from the core was stuck open. Water was leaking out.

Operators did not know this open valve was draining water from the core.

Pumps were switched on in an effort to get more water flowing. But in another part of the system, there were other valves that were closed when they should have been open. Operators in the control room did not realize this. Their view of one of these valve indicators was blocked by a hanging tag. Another indicator went unseen because an operator was leaning over the panel in front of it.[2]

Early on the morning of March 28, 1979, alarms sounded through the Unit 2 control room at Three Mile Island. Hundreds of lights flashed on the room's control panels.

Because of this, the accident progressed for another eight minutes. The water level was dropping and the temperature in the core was rising. When operators finally noticed the indicators showing that some valves were still closed, they immediately opened them. But the confusing series of alarms had misled them.

The control room indicators said that the water level in the reactor core was too high. Operators responded by trying to lower the water level. But the indicators read high only because of the water leaking through the one valve that was still stuck open. The operators still did not know it was stuck. They were trying to drain more water from the core when its water level was already too low.

By 6:00 A.M., at least fifty plant workers were in the control room trying to figure out what was wrong. A new set of alarms then warned the operators that low-level radiation was detected in the containment building that housed the reactor core. A short time later, another alarm warned of radiation in the control room itself. Technical duty officer George Kunder and shift supervisor William Zewe declared a site emergency. This meant there was danger of a radiation leak.[3]

Two hours and twenty-two minutes after the beginning of the accident, the open valve in the reactor core was discovered and closed. But the alarms about radiation levels in the containment building told the operators that they were too late.

The low water level in the core had allowed the uranium fuel rods to get too hot, and they had begun to melt. The melting fuel rods released dangerous amounts of radiation into the air around the core. If the rods continued to melt, they would become hot enough to burn through the floor of the reactor. The harm caused by such a "meltdown" would be deadly—and would be felt far beyond Three Mile Island.

The plant's personnel were now following their emergency plan. An emergency control station was set up inside the control room of the Unit 1 reactor. This reactor was shut down for refueling at the time. Operators reported the emergency to Pennsylvania's Department of Environmental Resources and the regional office of the Nuclear Regulatory Commission (NRC). The NRC is the federal government agency in charge of safety for nuclear power plants.

Plant Supervisor Gary Miller arrived in the Unit 2 control room shortly after 7:00 A.M. Minutes later, radiation levels in the unit's auxiliary building required that all personnel be evacuated from that area.

Nuclear engineer William Dornsife heard the evacuation order over the loudspeaker. "And I said to myself, 'This is the biggie,'" he recalled.[4]

At 7:24 A.M., Miller declared that the Three Mile Island Unit 2 reactor was under a general emergency, which meant that there was a possibility of danger to the public. The operators in the control room put on respirators, or breathing masks, to protect them from breathing any air contaminated with radiation. At that time, radiation levels inside the containment dome (the protective dome around the reactor core) had reached 10,000 rems per hour. Any human being exposed to that amount of radiation would die within minutes.[5]

The amount of water in the core was slowly rising back to a safe level. The containment building was automatically sealed. But radioactive water was still flowing through the pipes to the auxiliary building. Some of the pipes leaked, allowing radiation to escape.

In the control room, it was clear to Supervisor Gary Miller that the core had partially melted. The radiation levels told him so.

Police and firefighters in the nearby community of Middletown responded to the emergency. Radio station WKBO's news director Mike Pintek was alerted to the activity. Pintek called the plant to talk to a public relations official, but was put directly through to a man in the control room.

"I can't talk now, we've got a problem," the man said, and told Pintek to call Met Ed's headquarters in Reading, Pennsylvania. Pintek called and was assured that the accident posed no threat to the community.

"And that is the story we went with at 8:25 A.M.," Pintek later said. "I tried to tone it down so people wouldn't be alarmed."[6]

But people in the area were still scared. Pennsylvania Governor Richard Thornburgh assigned his Lieutenant Governor, William Scranton III, to oversee the state's response to the accident.

"There had never been anything like this," Scranton

Pennsylvania Governor Dick Thornburgh (left) and Lieutenant Governor William Scranton III discuss the Three Mile Island crisis at a press conference in March 1979.

later said. "It wasn't something you could feel or taste or touch. We were talking about radiation, which generated an enormous amount of fear."[7]

Scranton held a news conference that morning. Based on what he was told by Met Ed officials, he assured the public that the situation was under control. Moments after the conference, other officials from the company admitted to Scranton that the radiation leaks were worse than originally thought.

"It was at that point that I realized that we could not rely on Met Ed for the kind of information we needed to make decisions," Scranton recalled.[8]

Back in the control room, operators were still struggling to get the reactor's coolant system operating. Their efforts resulted in a hydrogen gas bubble forming at the top of the reactor chamber. The bubble was blocking the flow of water, so operators again decreased the flow to relieve pressure. Around 11:38 A.M., the water level in the core dropped so low that the uranium rods were again uncovered. Without the water, the rods became too hot. If the uranium fuel in the core remained uncovered, a meltdown would occur.

"The core could have turned into a molten, white hot mass, could have gone through the concrete base of the plant, and into ground water, which is immediately below the plant," said engineer and journalist Mike Gray. Such an event "could have fractured the earth [in the vicinity of the plant] in all directions, and geysers of radioactive steam would have spouted into the air through the parking lots, and a cloud of death would have wafted north over the city of Harrisburg."[9]

Such a serious meltdown threatened Three Mile Island if the problems in the Unit 2 reactor were not solved soon.

M et Ed Vice President Jack Herbein answers questions from reporters during a news conference in Hershey, Pennsylvania, on March 29, 1979.

CHAPTER 4

Crisis and Confusion

The national media began to gather at Three Mile Island's observation center early Wednesday afternoon, March 28, 1979. Met Ed Vice President Jack Herbein was chosen to speak to the press. He downplayed the seriousness of the accident. Many people in the community were concerned that Met Ed was hiding the truth about the accident. Mayor Robert Reid of Middletown was one of them.

"I was upset with the way things were being handled [by Met Ed]," Mayor Reid later said, "and the way we were being lied to."[1]

Herbein and other Met Ed officials met later in the afternoon with Lieutenant Governor Scranton. He called another press conference to update the public.

"Three Mile Island's situation is more complex than the company first led us to believe," Scranton said. The public grew more alarmed.[2]

NRC inspectors arrived at the plant. They were taken

to the turbine building. Inside, they saw workers in anticontamination suits, to protect them from radiation.

"This is an area of the plant that is normally not contaminated," recalled NRC inspector Jim Higgins. "It gave you the impression that there is something very wrong here."[3]

A telephone call finally got through to the control room from Babcock & Wilcox, the company that designed the plant. The designers urgently advised the operators to get water moving through the core. A short time later, operators switched the coolant system pumps back on. The water level rose, the fuel rods cooled, and the pressure stabilized. The crisis seemed to be over.

The communities around Three Mile Island waited impatiently Wednesday evening for answers about the accident. Meanwhile, the rest of the nation was becoming aware of what happened through television's evening news broadcasts. "A government official said that a breakdown in an atomic power plant in Pennsylvania today is probably the worst nuclear accident to date," reported Walter Cronkite on that night's CBS Evening News.[4]

On Thursday morning, Lieutenant Governor Scranton traveled to Three Mile Island to inspect the damage. He was put in a protective suit and taken into the plant's auxiliary building. There he saw water on the building's floor. The water looked normal, but Scranton knew it was highly contaminated with radiation. Seeing no signs of emergency or panic, he was encouraged by the visit.

He reported to Governor Thornburgh that the situation appeared under control.

But throughout the day, Governor Thornburgh received conflicting reports from Three Mile Island, the NRC, and Pennsylvania's Emergency Management Agency. No one could tell him how much radiation had been released. Thornburgh was reluctant to call for any sort of evacuation of the area around the plant. Unless the professionals at Three Mile Island and the NRC could agree

*P*ennsylvania state police stand outside the closed front gate of the Three Mile Island plant in March 1979. The plant was shut down while officials tried to avoid a nuclear disaster.

that an evacuation was necessary, Thornburgh wanted to avoid causing a panic.

"I believe, at this point, that there is no cause for alarm," Thornburgh said to reporters Thursday afternoon. "I realize that you are being subjected to a conflicting array of information from a wide variety of sources. So am I. I spent virtually the entire last 36 hours trying to separate fact from fiction about this situation. I feel that we have succeeded on the more important questions."[5]

But the confusion surrounding the release of radiation grew worse the following morning, Friday, March 30. Conflicting reports about radiation levels outside the plant led NRC officials to advise Governor Thornburgh to recommend an evacuation of people as far as ten miles downwind from Three Mile Island. Officials at Met Ed alerted the emergency preparedness offices in the surrounding counties that an evacuation order was going to be issued. A warning of a possible evacuation was announced over a local radio station.

In the meantime, NRC officials learned that the reported level of radiation released outside the plant was in error, due to a mix-up in communications. After learning this, NRC Chairman Joseph Hendrie called Governor Thornburgh shortly after 10:00 A.M. He informed the governor that no evacuation was needed. Hendrie instead advised that everyone within five miles of the plant should stay indoors for the next half hour.

Thornburgh and his staff were not sure what to do. The information the governor had been getting from the

NRC had been confusing and unreliable. If there really was danger, hundreds of thousands of people would have to be evacuated. But an evacuation order also presented risks to the safety of the people in the area. While Thornburgh struggled with the decision, he suddenly heard an air raid siren ring throughout the city.

"That siren was like a knife in my chest," Thornburgh recalled. "I thought, 'What on Earth? Where did that come from?'" Someone in Harrisburg had set off the siren, but never came forward. Although it rang for no official reason, its ringing added to the tension in the city.[6]

A short time later, Thornburgh received a call from President Jimmy Carter. The President understood nuclear reactors well. He had served as an officer aboard a nuclear submarine during his years in the U.S. Navy. Carter informed Thornburgh that he was sending Harold Denton to Three Mile Island. Denton was director of nuclear reactor regulation at the NRC. He was to serve as an expert adviser to Thornburgh. Denton was to assist the governor in dealing with the crisis and speaking to the press. He could not get there soon enough.

Tensions grew during a press conference at 11:00 A.M. Friday morning. As emotions ran high, Jack Herbein was unprepared for the aggressive questioning from reporters.

"I remember feeling very angry," radio reporter Mike Pintek later said. "I shouted a question to Jack Herbein. 'You started to melt that thing down, didn't you! Didn't you!' I guess at that moment I wasn't a journalist anymore . . . I lived here, and I was mad."[7]

At 12:30 that afternoon, Governor Thornburgh advised pregnant women and preschool children within a five-mile radius of Three Mile Island to leave the area. The governor also closed all schools within that area. After the governor's warning, pregnant women and small children were not the only ones who left. Many others feared the dangers were far worse than they were being told, and decided to leave the area.[8]

Marsha McHenry was one of the more than 140,000 people who left the area over the next four days. Her neighbors invited her to their house and explained to her that nothing was going to stop them from leaving. They had guns, a chainsaw, and a big truck. McHenry said

The streets of Goldsboro, Pennsylvania, were like those of a ghost town after being abandoned almost completely in the wake of the accident at Three Mile Island in 1979.

they planned to get out on the highway, cut down any barriers they encountered, and get away.

"So the idea that there was going to be any kind of an orderly evacuation," McHenry said, "was pure fantasy."[9]

Harold Denton and his team of experts from NRC headquarters arrived at Three Mile Island at 2:00 P.M. Friday. They were immediately faced with a new problem. The experts already knew that a large bubble of hydrogen gas had been created inside the reactor. When hydrogen comes in contact with the oxygen in the air, the smallest spark can cause it to explode, much like gasoline. Such an explosion would blow the reactor core open and allow a

*H*arold Denton, director of the Nuclear Regulatory Commission (NRC), was sent by President Carter to act as a special advisor to Governor Thornburgh during the Three Mile Island crisis.

large amount of harmful radiation to spread to the surrounding area.

Based on estimates he had received before leaving NRC headquarters, Denton believed the hydrogen bubble would not become explosive for another five to eight days. He believed there was plenty of time to get the bubble out of the reactor core before it became explosive.

Not until 8:30 P.M. did Denton meet with Governor Thornburgh in person. He told the governor that there was extensive fuel damage within the reactor. He said that the hydrogen bubble within the core was being worked on, and that there was no need to call for an evacuation. The two men then held a press conference to update the public on the accident.

President Carter had sent the right man. Harold Denton's expertise and personality helped put everyone at ease. After Denton spoke to the governor and the media, it seemed that the situation was finally under control.[10]

Another NRC engineer, Roger Mattson, was not convinced. Back at NRC headquarters, in Bethesda, Maryland, he had analyzed some control room data from Three Mile Island. The data told him that the hydrogen gas bubble was in immediate danger to explode. He spoke to Chairman Hendrie by phone late Friday evening.[11]

"How do we get the bubble out of there?" Mattson wondered aloud. "I don't know what we're protecting at this point. I think we ought to be moving people."[12]

CHAPTER 5

Calming the Crisis

On Saturday morning, March 31, 1979, Chairman Hendrie advised Roger Mattson to get answers on the dangers of the hydrogen bubble. Mattson talked to the best nuclear physicists in the country. Within hours, the advice he received was that the bubble was already at an explosive level. It could blow up at any time.

Meanwhile, Harold Denton's team near Three Mile Island had gathered different data. Led by NRC engineer Victor Stello, the group of experts at the facility believed that there was no explosive potential at all. They were convinced that there was no immediate danger.

But who was right?

Lives depended upon the correct answer to that question. Word of the ongoing debate between the two teams of engineers leaked to the media. At a press conference in Harrisburg on Saturday night, Denton and Governor Thornburgh sought to clear up the matter.

Thornburgh assured reporters "there is no imminent

catastrophic event foreseeable at the Three Mile Island facility."[1]

"There is not a combustible (explosive) mixture in the containment or in the reactor vessel," Denton said. "And there is no near-term danger at all."

Reporters asked Denton whether there was still disagreement between the teams of engineers. "No, there is no disagreement," Denton replied. "I guess it is the way things get presented."[2]

*E*ngineer Victor Stello (below) was one of the NRC experts who believed that there was no immediate threat of a nuclear explosion at Three Mile Island.

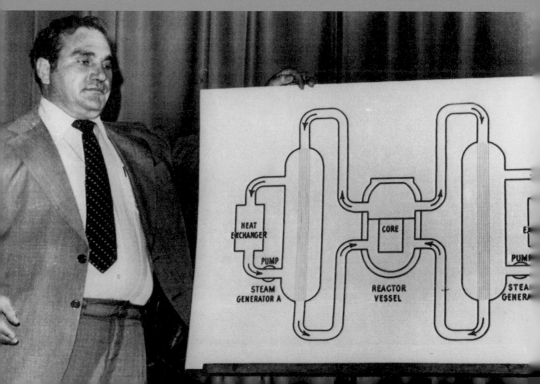

But there was disagreement and Denton knew it. He wanted to calm the public's concerns because he was confident that his own team of engineers was correct.

"We believed the people on-site," said Lt. Gov. Scranton, who was also present at the press conference. "And Harold Denton was the guy we trusted most by this time."[3]

There was another reason Denton wanted to calm the public's concern. During the press conference, Governor Thornburgh announced that President Carter would arrive the following day.

President Carter believed the emergency had reached a level at which Americans were looking to him for leadership. If Denton's team was right, then the President's visit would occur as scheduled, and hopefully have a calming effect on the crisis. If his team was wrong, President Carter would be exposing himself to a very dangerous situation.

Carter planned to visit the facility on the morning of Sunday, April 1. As Carter flew by helicopter from Washington, D.C., to Harrisburg that morning, the debate over the dangers of the hydrogen bubble in the core had not yet been settled.

Roger Mattson arrived at the Harrisburg airport shortly before the President. He and Victor Stello immediately got into a heated argument over the core's condition. Stello was the engineer who had been advising Harold Denton that the bubble presented no danger. When the President arrived, Denton briefed him on the two opinions

President Jimmy Carter (center) inspects the Three Mile Island control room along with NRC Director Harold Denton (left) on April 1, 1979, four days after the accident.

about the danger of the bubble. President Carter did not believe he could turn back.

Accompanied by Governor Thornburgh and Harold Denton, Carter rode in his motorcade to the facility. All along the route through Middletown, people came out of their homes and lined the streets to see the President.

"People weren't talking to each other," said Middletown Mayor Robert Reid. "They were cooped up in their homes, and when he came by, it seemed like everyone came out to see the president, and it was really a shot in the arm."[4]

Carter entered the facility and visited Unit 2's control

room, the scene of much chaos and fear four days earlier. Followed by news cameras, the president spoke with several workers at the plant before departing.

Before Carter left from the Harrisburg airport, Victor Stello discovered that Mattson's scientific team had incorrectly calculated the risk posed by the hydrogen bubble. There was no immediate danger of it exploding.

President Carter left the Harrisburg airport that afternoon. His visit had helped to calm many fears about potential dangers at the plant. Over the following days, plant operators allowed the hydrogen bubble to slowly and safely leak away from the core. The radiation seemed to be contained. The emergency appeared to be over.[5]

Schools reopened and the people who had left the area around Three Mile Island returned to their communities. On April 9, 1979, the crisis was declared over.

CHAPTER 6

The Legacy of Three Mile Island

In October 1979, the NRC fined Metropolitan Edison $155,000 for their mismanagement of the crisis at Three Mile Island. But Met Ed was not the only one at fault. The NRC itself was partly to blame for what led to the accident.

"They (the NRC and the nuclear power industry) scaled this thing up from the 100 megawatt demonstration plants to these 1,000 megawatt superplants like Three Mile Island without anything in between," said engineer and journalist Mike Gray. "These monster plants were something they did not understand clearly."[1]

The pressure relief valve that failed at Three Mile Island had failed eleven previous times at other plants. But neither the plant's designer nor the NRC had tried to correct the valve design. They did not even issue a warning.

"That warning, if it had gone out and been received by all the rest of the similar nuclear power plants, then the accident at Three Mile Island would never have happened," Gray added.[2]

The President's Commission on the accident cited poor training of the plant operators as the key factor in the accident. They recommended dozens of changes in the operation and regulation of nuclear power plants. These changes included an expansion of the NRC's inspection program. They also included upgrading safety requirements in plant design and equipment. They urged better training for plant operators. They also called for improved instruments in control rooms.[3]

Cleanup operations over the years have shown that the damage at Three Mile Island was worse than originally thought. In July 1982, cleanup workers discovered dozens of melted fuel rods at the bottom of the reactor's containment vessel.

There had definitely been a meltdown at Three Mile Island.

In 1986, seven years after the Three Mile Island crisis, a far worse accident occurred. It happened at the Chernobyl Nuclear Reactor in the Ukraine, then part of the former Soviet Union. What had

This picture was taken from a television monitor at the Three Mile Island facility in 1983. It shows the broken fuel rods at the bottom of the Unit 2 reactor.

A protest to commemorate the twentieth anniversary of the accident at Three Mile Island was held just outside the plant in March 1999.

been feared at Three Mile Island actually took place at Chernobyl. The plant's Number 4 reactor exploded, shooting flames and leaking deadly radiation into the air. The land for miles around the plant was contaminated. Approximately 49,000 people were evacuated. Their homes will remain uninhabitable for many years because of the radiation.[4]

So far, the most significant legacy of Three Mile Island is that no new orders for the construction of nuclear power plants have been placed since the accident in 1979. For more than twenty years, no nuclear power plants have been built.

Television correspondent Robert Hager remembered arriving at the airport in Harrisburg to cover the accident for NBC News. The moment he stepped off the plane was the same moment the air raid siren in Harrisburg had been mysteriously turned on.

"As for that first siren," Hager later said, "it may have

The cooling towers of Three Mile Island's Unit 2 reactor (right), and the towers of Unit 1 (left). The Unit 2 reactor has not been used since the accident in 1979. Unit 1 remains in operation, however.

been a sort of false alarm at the time. But long-term, it sounded an end to an era when we believed that nuclear power would be the answer to the world's energy problems."[5]

New technologies may someday help produce nuclear power in a way that is safer and more acceptable to the public. Only time will tell whether these technologies prove successful enough to prevent another disaster like the one at Three Mile Island.

Other Nuclear Accidents

DATE	PLACE	DESCRIPTION
December 12, 1952	Ottawa, Canada	A partial meltdown occurs after four control rods are mistakenly removed from a reactor's core. Millions of gallons of radioactive water accumulate within the reactor. Fortunately, there are no serious injuries.
September 29, 1957	Kyshtym, Soviet Union	Radioactive wastes at a nuclear weapons factory explode. More than 10,000 people forced to evacuate the contaminated area.
October 10, 1957	Liverpool, England	Fire in the Windscale Pile No. 1 reactor causes radiation to blow out across the surrounding land. A two-hundred-square-mile area is contaminated.
1976	Greifswald, East Germany	A near-meltdown occurs at the Lubmin nuclear power plant when safety systems fail during a fire.
April 26, 1986	Chernobyl, Soviet Union	An explosion within a reactor core causes a tremendous amount of radiation to be released. It spreads over parts of the Soviet Union, Europe, and Scandinavia. Thirty-one deaths, though estimates of radiation casualties run into the thousands.
September 30, 1999	Tokaimura, Japan	Chain reaction within a uranium-processing plant runs out of control. Radioactive gas is released, exposing sixty-nine people. One worker is killed and two others are seriously injured.

Chapter 1. General Emergency

1. People and Events: Mike Pintek, "Meltdown at Three Mile Island," *PBS Online*, n.d. <http://www.pbs.org/wgbh/amex/three/peopleevents/pandeAMEX89.html> (July 26, 2000).

2. People and Events: Dick Thornburgh, "Meltdown at Three Mile Island," *PBS Online*, n.d. <http://www.pbs.org/wgbh/amex/three/peopleevents/pandeAMEX97.html> (July 26, 2000).

Chapter 2. The Nuclear Age

1. Tony Rothman, *Instant Physics* (New York: Fawcett Columbine, 1995), pp.150–156.

2. Electric Library, "Nuclear Energy," Encyclopedia.com, n.d. <http://www.encyclopedia.com/articles/09401.html> (November 8, 2000).

3. Timeline of Nuclear Technology, "Meltdown at Three Mile Island," *PBS Online*, n.d. <http://www.pbs.org/wgbh/amex/three/timeline/index.html> (July 26, 2000).

Chapter 3. Meltdown

1. Nuclear Issues Briefing Paper, "Three Mile Island: 1979," *Uranium Information Center; Ltd.*, June 2000, <http://www.uic.com.au/nip48.htm> (July 26, 2000).

2. PBS Home Video, "The American Experience: Meltdown At Three Mile Island," WGBH Educational Foundation, 1999.

3. President's Commission Report, "Three Mile Island Nuclear Accident: Day 1," *Three Mile Island Alert, Inc.*, nd. <http://www.enviroweb.org/trnial28.html> (June 15, 2000).

4. Ibid.

5. PBS Home Video, "The American Experience: Meltdown at Three Mile Island," WGBH Educational Foundation, 1999.

6. President's Commission Report.

7. People and Events: William Scranton, "Meltdown at Three Mile Island," *PBS Online*, n.d. <http://www.pbs.org/wgbh/amex/three/peopleevents/pandeAMEX96.html> (July 26, 2000).

8. Ibid.

9. PBS Home Video.

Chapter 4. Crisis and Confusion

1. People and Events: Robert Reid, "Meltdown at Three Mile Island," *PBS Online*, n.d. <http://www.pbs.org/wgbh/amex/three/peopleevents/pandeAMEX90.html> (July 26, 2000).

2. President's Commission Report, "Three Mile Island Nuclear Accident: Day 1," *Three Mile Island Alert, Inc.*, n.d. <http://www.enviroweb.org/tmia/28.html> (June 15, 2000).

3. PBS Home Video, "The American Experience: Meltdown at Three Mile Island," WGBH Educational Foundation, 1999.

4. President's Commission Report.

5. People and Events: Dick Thornburgh, "Meltdown at Three Mile Island," *PBS Online*, n.d. <http://www.pbs.org/wgbh/amex/three/peopleevents/pandeAMEX97.html> (July 26, 2000).

6. Ibid.

7. PBS Home Video.

8. Nuclear Issues Briefing Paper, "Three Mile Island: 1979," *Uranium Information Center, Ltd.*, June 2000, <http://www.uic.com.au/nip48.htm> (July 26, 2000).

9. PBS Home Video.

10. People and Events: Harold Denton, "Meltdown at Three Mile Island," *PBS Online*, n.d. <http://www.pbs.org/wgbh/amex/three/peopleevents/pandeAMEX89.html> (July 26, 2000).

11. President's Commission Report, "Three Mile Island Nuclear Accident: Day 4," *Three Mile Island Alert, Inc.*, n.d. <http://www.enviroweb.org/tmia/31.html> (June 15, 2000).

12. PBS Home Video.

Chapter 5. Calming the Crisis

1. President's Commission Report, "Three Mile Island Nuclear Accident: Day 4," *Three Mile Island Alert, Inc.*, n.d. <http://www.enviroweb.org/trnia/31.html> (June 15, 2000).

2. Ibid.

3. PBS Home Video, "The American Experience: Meltdown at Three Mile Island," WGBH Educational Foundation, 1999.

4. People and Events: Jimmy Carter, "Meltdown at Three Mile Island," *PBS Online*, n.d. <http://www.pbs.org/wgbh/amex/three/peopleevents/pandeAMEX86.html> (July 26, 2000).

5. Nuclear Issues Briefing Paper, "Three Mile Island: 1979," *Uranium Information Center; Ltd.*, June 2000, <http://www.uic.com.au/nip48.htm> (July 26, 2000).

Chapter 6. The Legacy of Three Mile Island

1. PBS Home Video, "The American Experience: Meltdown at Three Mile Island," WGBH Educational Foundation, 1999.

2. Ibid.

3. "Three Mile Island 2 Accident," *Nuclear Regulatory Commission Home Page*, n.d. <http://www.nrc.gov/OPA/gmo/tip/tmi.htm> (July 26, 2000).

4. Piers Paul Read, Ablaze: The Story of Chernobyl (New York: Random House, 1993), pp.132–290.

5. Robert Hager, "A Reporter Remembers Three Mile Island," *MSNBC.com*, n.d. <http://www.msnbc.com/news/253397.asp> (July 26, 2000).

Glossary

atoms—The smallest particles that make up the chemical elements.

chain reaction—A series of events where each action initiates the next.

core—The central structure of a nuclear reactor, in which the energy-producing fission reactions occur.

electrons—Negatively charged subatomic particles that orbit around the nucleus of an atom.

fission—An energy-producing process in which atomic nuclei are split into particles that in turn split other nuclei, continuing in a chain reaction. Nuclear reactor cores contain fission reactions.

hydrogen—The simplest and most common element in nature.

meltdown— A nuclear disaster in which the nuclear fuel in a reactor melts and burns through the reactor's containment structure and into the ground, contaminating the environment.

neutrons—Neutrally charged subatomic particles that make up part of the nucleus of an atom.

nuclear energy—Energy produced by splitting atomic nuclei.

nuclear reactor—A device in which nuclear reactions are produced.

nucleus—The central part of an atom, containing protons and neutrons.

protons—Positively charged subatomic particles that, along with neutrons, make up the nucleus of an atom.

radiation—The particles or rays given off by an unstable atom.

uranium—A silver-colored, radioactive metal. One of the heaviest and most complex elements in nature.

Condon, Judith. *Chernobyl & Other Nuclear Accidents.* Austin, Tex.: Raintree Steck-Vaughn Publishers, 1999.

De Angelis, Therese. *Three Mile Island.* Broomall, Pa.: Chelsea House Publishers, 2001.

Helgerson, Joel. *Nuclear Accidents.* New York, N.Y.: Franklin Watts, Inc., 1988.

Marx, Trish and Beh-Eger, Dorita. *I Heal: The Children of Chernobyl in Cuba.* Minneapolis, Minn.: The Lerner Publishing Group, 1996.

Morgan, Nina. *Nuclear Power.* Austin, Tex.: Raintree Steck-Vaughn Publishers, 1997.

Pirani, F. *What's the Big Idea?: Nuclear Power.* London, England: Hodder & Stoughton, Limited, 1999.

Ward, Pat and Ward, Barb. *Nuclear Energy.* Lewistown, Mo.: M. Twain Media Incorporated Publishers, 1999.

Wilcox, Charlotte. *Powerhouse: Inside a Nuclear Power Plant.* Minneapolis, Minn.: The Lerner Publishing Group, 1996.

Meltdown at Three Mile Island
http://www.pbs.org/wgbh/amex/three/

Three Mile Island
http://www.encyclopedia.com/articles/12843.html

Three Mile Island Control Room
http://www.tmia.com/croom.htm

The Hiroshima Peace Site
http://www.pcf.city.hiroshima.jp/peacesite/indexE.html

Index

A
atomic bombs, 7, 9, 10
Atomic Energy Act, 9, 13
atoms, 11, 12
B
Babcock and Wilcox
    Company, 13, 24
C
Carter, President Jimmy, 27,
    33, 34
Chernobyl, 37, 38
Cronkite, Walter, 24
D
Denton, Harold, 27, 29,
    30–33, 34
E
"Energy Crisis," 12
F
fission, 11
G
Gray, Mike, 21, 36, 37
H
Hager, Robert, 39, 40
Hendrie, Joseph, 26, 31
Herbein, Jack, 22, 23, 27
M
Matson, Roger, 30, 31, 33, 35
McHenry, Marsha, 28, 29
Metropolitan Edison
    Company, 7, 8, 13, 20, 23,
    26, 36
Miller, Gary, 18, 19
N
nuclear power
    history, 9, 12
    description, 11, 12
    previous accidents, 12
Nuclear Regulatory
    Commission (NRC), 18,
    25–27, 29, 30, 36, 37
O
OPEC, 12, 13

P
Pintek, Mike, 7, 19
R
Reid, Robert, 23, 34
S
Scranton, William III, 19, 20,
    23–25, 33
Stello, Victor, 31, 32, 33, 35
T
Thornburgh, Richard, 8, 19,
    20, 25–27, 30–33, 34
Three Mile Island nuclear
    accident
    aftermath, 36, 37–40
    arrival of Harold Denton, 29
    arrival of NRC inspectors, 24
    beginning of accident, 15–17
    Carter's visit, 33, 34, 35
    discovery of partial
        core-melt, 19
    evacuation recommended,
        26–28
    general emergency
        declared, 18
    government's first
        reaction, 20
    hydrogen bubble
        controversy, 30–33
    hydrogen gas bubble
        develops, 21
    Lt. Gov. Scranton inspects
        damage, 24
    Met Ed's first response to
        accident, 22, 23
    plant design and
        construction, 13
    prelude to accident, 13, 14
Truman, Harry, 9, 13
U
uranium, 11, 12